England

# CURIOUS CREATURES
# IN PECULIAR PLACES

Written and illustrated by
Amy Goldman Koss

PRICE STERN SLOAN
Los Angeles

Published by Price Stern Sloan, Inc.
360 North La Cienega Boulevard, Los Angeles,
California 90048

ISBN: 0-8431-2732-5

10 9 8 7 6 5 4 3 2 1

**Library of Congress Cataloging-in-Publication Data**

Koss, Amy Goldman, 1954-
    Curious creatures in peculiar places / written and illustrated by
Amy Goldman Koss.
        p.    cm.
    Summary: Describes, in rhyming text and illustrations, the
habitats and characteristics of a variety of unusual animals.
     ISBN (invalid) 08431027325 : $8.95 ($12.95 Can.)
     1. Rare animals—Juvenile literature.
Animals      I. Title.
QL83.K67    1989
591'.042—dc19
                           89-3847
                           CIP
                           AC

**To Lisa Endig and Rusty Strickstein**

**1.** ELF OWL: *Sonora Desert, North America.* **2.** TREE CRAB: *Jamaica, West Indies.* **3.** SLOTH: *Costa Rica, Panama, Colombia, Venezuela—Central and South America.* **4.** ALPACA: *Andes Mountains, Bolivia and Peru—South America.* **5.** AUK: *Arctic Coast, Greenland.* **6.** FIRE-BELLIED TOAD: *Finland, Siberia—Northern Europe.* **7.** OKAPI: *Zaire, Africa.* **8.** MANDRILL: *Cameroon, West Africa.* **9.** MEERKAT: *Kalahari Desert, Botswana—South Africa.* **10.** JACKSON'S CHAMELEON: *Kenya, East Africa.* **11.** CHINESE PANGOLIN: *China, Nepal—Asia.* **12.** NARWHAL: *Arctic Ocean.* **13.** TARSIER: *Sumatra, Celebes—Indonesia; Borneo.* **14.** DUCKBILL PLATYPUS: *Tasmania, Australia.*

*1. North America*

# ELF OWL

Out here in the desert
There's not much around.
A few prickly cactus
Stick out of the ground.

A hole in the cactus,
As odd as it seems,
Is home to an elf owl,
Deep in his dreams.

His nest in the cactus
Is shady and cool,
While out in the sunshine
The heat is so cruel.

He sleeps there inside
Through the hot desert day
And comes out at twilight
To eat and to play.

He sounds like a puppy;
He yips and he whines
And barks to his mate as
The desert moon shines.

2. West Indies

# TREE CRAB

The island of Jamaica
Has plants that stick to trees.
They cling as if by magic
To any tree they please.

Each has a little pocket
To capture fallen rain.
This miniature aquarium's
A cozy crab domain.

This crab is flat and tiny
So he can scoot around.
He'll spend his life on just one plant
And never touch the ground.

Jamaica's warm and breezy;
The crab's life looks like fun.
He splashes in his leafy pool,
Then snoozes in the sun.

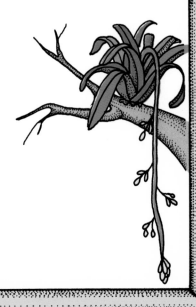

3. Central and South America

# SLOTH

The shy, timid sloth, way up in the trees
Lives peacefully on her own.
She hangs upside-down from her toes eating leaves
In Panama's tropical zone.

Algae grow green on her thick, bushy hair
As she hangs wrong-side-up in her tree.
The algae blend in with her colors up there
And make the sloth harder to see.

But better than hiding so well among leaves,
The sloth's most unusual skill
Is that she attracts no attention at all
By keeping remarkably still.

The sloth will remain there for hours and hours
To eat all she can from one spot.
She's bathed every day by the rain forest showers,
Which cool her right down when she's hot.

4. South America

# ALPACA

In the Andes mountains,
Which cut across Peru,
Alpacas graze contentedly
On grasses called ichu.

They store food in their tummies
To help them to get by
When mountain grass is hard to find
And streams are running dry.

Their coats are long and shaggy;
They're toasty all the time.
And when the slopes are slippery
Their spiked hooves help them climb.

They never mind the weather
Or cold, thin mountain air;
They're perfectly adapted so
They do just fine up there.

5. Greenland

# AUK*

Some birds can swim, some dive, some fly,
And some can only walk.
One arctic bird does all these things:
The chubby little auk.

Auks love each other's company.
They hate to be alone.
So millions of them claim one cliff
And call its crags their home.

These crowded, noisy cliffs stand tall
Against the arctic sky.
It's windy and it's cold up there.
No neighbors live nearby.

They fly together to the sea
And dive for fish to eat.
To swim around beneath the waves,
They flap their wings and feet.

The auks live in a dreary place,
With bitter winds and ice.
But they don't miss green grass or trees;
They think cold rocks are nice.

*also called dovekie

*6. Northern Europe*

# FIRE-BELLIED TOAD

Winters last longer and summers are cool
In the land of the midnight sun.
The toad has to hibernate most of the year
And has just a few weeks for fun.

When she comes hopping out late in the spring
She's ready to eat and to breed.
But hungry young birds who are waiting out there
Are also quite eager to feed.

Birds think that toads are just yummy to eat
But this is the wrong toad to pick.
Because if a bird eats the fire-bellied toad
That bird will get terribly sick.

How do birds know that this plump little toad
Is not the right toad to attack?
Because they are warned by the bright underside
That shows when she arches her back.

Red and black patterns mean dangerous things.
They mean she is poison to eat.
Since animals know what this color code means
They see red and black and retreat.

7. Africa

# OKAPI*

Okapis make no sound at all
And forests kept them covered,
And that is why it took so long
For them to be discovered.

Okapis look like zebras but
More detailed information
Has shown giraffes are actually
Much closer in relation.

Okapis have giraffe-like horns
And tongues for plucking leaves.
It's just coincidence that gives
Them stripy zebra sleeves.

Their necks are shorter than giraffes',
But limber for their size.
They lick themselves all over while
They flick their tails at flies.

These gentle vegetarians,
So mild and sweet and shy,
Can buck and kick when they're alarmed
Their heels fly hard and high.

*pronounced: oh-copy

8. West Africa

# MANDRILL

The mandrill likes variety.
He eats the jungle fruits.
He also likes to snack on snakes
And lizards, snails and roots.

Together with his relatives
He'll pass a lazy day
And groom and grunt quite happily
Till trouble comes his way.

When danger's near he bares his teeth.
His fangs are sharp and long.
He beats the earth to warn his foe
That he is mean and strong.

His hair stands up around his neck
He makes an awful sound,
His chest turns blue, his wrists turn red
That's how he stands his ground.

His enemies are terrified
And run away in fright.
So rarely does the mandrill male
Really have to fight.

9. South Africa

# MEERKAT

The Kalahari Desert is
Where meerkats scratch and scramble
To stay alive on drifting sands
With rocks and thorny bramble.

Their life is rough, the desert's harsh
And peril's always near.
For there are foxes, hawks and snakes
And other things to fear.

They work together as a team
And share their chores all day.
Some hunt, some guard, some babysit;
It's fair to all that way.

Each takes a turn at every task.
Their system is unique.
The one who stands on guard can warn
The others with a squeak.

The babysitters quickly get
The children out of sight.
While older meerkats face their foe
And get prepared to fight.

When day is done, back in their den,
They frolic in a heap.
They cuddle and they hug and play
Until they fall asleep.

10. East Africa

# JACKSON'S CHAMELEON

Chameleon babies start their lives
By running from their mother.
She gets so hungry when they're born
She'd eat one or another.

She changes colors in the light;
Now yellow, green or grey.
It's hard to spot her in the wild;
She sneaks around that way.

She also hides by changing shape
To look just like a twig.
Or when she wants to fool someone
She puffs up really big.

Her tongue is more than twice as long
As all the rest of her.
She catches bugs so fast with it,
It passes in a blur.

Her eyes can watch two ways at once.
Not much escapes her gaze.
An insect doesn't stand a chance
Against her tricky ways.

# CHINESE PANGOLIN*

His spiky scales look dangerous
And difficult to eat.
He's prickly as a pine cone or
An artichoke with feet.

Although his scales and claws are sharp,
He will not fight at all.
Instead he curls himself up in
A spiny, armored ball.

He sprays an icky smell and he
Can make a hissing sound.
He runs around on his hind legs,
His front feet off the ground.

He claws at trees and anthills where
The ants and termites hide.
He pokes his sticky tongue in there
And licks around inside.

He shuts his eyes and ears and nose
To eat these wiggly treats,
So insects who can sting and bite
Won't hurt him while he eats.

*also called spiny anteater

12. Arctic Ocean

# NARWHAL

Up in the icy polar sea
There lives a unicorn
Whose spiral spear is one long tooth
Which looks just like a horn.

He and his friends will use their spears
To spar and fence in play.
It's just in fun but they impress
The narwhal girls that way.

His spear's the only tooth he has
And so he cannot chew.
He swallows fish and squid up whole
Like vacuum cleaners do.

He looks just like a giant fish,
But has no gills or scales.
He has mammalian lungs and fur
Just like all other whales.

You'd think that he would catch a chill
Up in that frigid sea,
But thanks to all his blubber he's
As comfy as can be.

13. Indonesia and Borneo

# TARSIER*

This Indonesian goblin
Has great big, googly eyes
And hands that move so quickly they
Can even capture flies.

With padded sticky fingers
He clings to twig and vine.
His head can twist around as if
He had a rubber spine.

His large, round amber eyeballs
Can see quite well at night.
Each eye outweighs his brain and so
He isn't very bright.

He's constantly in motion,
Just leaping here to there.
This makes him seem to pop right out
Of nothing but thin air.

The island people feared him.
They thought his jumpy ways
Were proof he was an evil ghost
Who'd haunt them all their days.

*pronounced tar-zee-ay

14. Australia

# DUCKBILL PLATYPUS

The platypus is quite a weird
Australian fuzzy beast;
Her beaver tail and duck-like bill
Are odd to say the least.

She scurries on her fat, webbed feet
And waddles like a duck.
She digs long burrows in the dirt
And paddles in the muck.

To hide inside her burrow is
Among her greatest joys.
Her hearing is so keen that she
Could die because of noise.

Her eyes are weak but she can sniff
So well with her long snout
That even under water she
Can smell the fishes out.

She is the only mammal who
Lays eggs as reptiles do.
Her babies ride inside her pouch
Just like the kangaroo.

The platypus is delicate
And not the type to roam.
She can't adapt to life in zoos
Or live away from home.

**Special thanks to:**
1. The Los Angeles Zoo
2. The Natural History Museum of Los Angeles County
3. Mitchell Koss
4, 5, & 6. Max, Harriet and Barry Goldman

*North America*